IMAGES
of America

EAST NASHVILLE

Best Wishes —
Michael Fleenor

IMAGES
of America

EAST NASHVILLE

E. Michael Fleenor

ARCADIA

Published by Arcadia Publishing,
an imprint of Tempus Publishing, Inc.
2 Cumberland Street
Charleston, SC 29401

Printed in Great Britain.

Library of Congress Catalog Card Number: 98-87327

For all general information contact Arcadia Publishing at:
Telephone 843-853-2070
Fax 843-853-0044
E-Mail arcadia@charleston.net

For customer service and orders:
Toll-Free 1-888-313-BOOK

Visit us on the internet at http://www.arcadiaimages.com

For George Graham
and for my Lockeland Springs neighbors
who have made East Nashville such a special place for me.

CONTENTS

ACKNOWLEDGMENTS

The author wishes to thank Mary Glenn Hearne and the staff of the Nashville Room of the Ben West Library, Ken Feith and the staff of the Metro Nashville Archives, Barry McCallister at Metro Parks, and all the librarians at the Tennessee State Library and Archives who have given assistance to me in this endeavor. I'd also like to thank my colleague at the Tennessee Historical Commission, Steve Rogers, for his help, as well as all of the persons who generously shared photographs and memories of East Nashville with me: Ashley Caldwell of the H.G. Hill Company; Amelia Whittsett Edwards; Mac Hill; Mr. and Mrs. Bud Lehning; Robert Oermann; Bessie Redmon; James Vester Jr; Rick Warwick; the East Branch Carnegie Library; Historic Edgefield, Inc.; the Lockeland Springs Neighborhood Association; the Trevecca University Archives; and the congregations of East End United Methodist Church, Eastwood Christian Church, First Church of the Nazarene, Holy Name Catholic Church, St. Ann's Episcopal Church, and Woodland Presbyterian Church.

PHOTO CREDITS:

East Branch Carnegie Library	EBL
Historic Edgefield, Inc.	HEI
Lockeland Springs Neighborhood Association	LSNA
Metro Nashville & Davidson Co. Archives	MNA
Metro Nashville Parks Department	MPD
Nashville Room, Ben West Library	NR
Tennessee State Library & Archives	TSLA
Trevecca Nazarene University Archives	TNUA

INTRODUCTION

East Nashville has maintained a somewhat separate identity from the city across the Cumberland River, of which it is a part. In this collection of photographs from the 1870s to 1961, I hope to convey to you some of East Nashville's rich history, to give you a glimpse at the area's homes, churches, schools, businesses, and parks, and of the people who lived, worked, studied, and relaxed here. My images are diverse, but I know that there are buildings and areas of East Nashville I have left out because images were not available. We will be looking only at Old East Nashville, or the area approximately from the river to Greenwood Avenue and from Ellington Parkway to Riverside Drive, and not at North Edgefield (northeast Nashville), South Inglewood, or the Rosebank areas.

Most of these images come from the Tennessee State Library & Archives, the Nashville Room of the Ben West Library, or the Metro Archives. Several photographs of individual houses and street scenes were used as court exhibits in cases involving automobile and/or trolley traffic accidents. A number of images of Shelby Park from the Metro Park Department have only been seen by a few individuals. Also, I was fortunate that a number of individuals and organizations shared their images with me. Images of Lockeland Mansion and bottling works were collected by Judi Wells and donated to the Metro Archives, East Branch Carnegie Library, and Lockeland Springs Neighborhood Association, all of whom graciously allowed me to reproduce them.

While I am saddened by the lost landmarks in these images, I'm also impressed at how much remains. Along with its architecture and sense of community, I think it is East Nashville's history and resilience that has made it attractive to young home buyers. As we approach the 21st century, this physical link to the 19th century makes the future feel safer. We are comforted by the idea that people 70 to 150 years ago were living, working, and studying in many of the same buildings we in East Nashville live, work, and study in today. I hope this book makes those people and places more special for you.

EDGEFIELD, 1860. "Nashville and the 16th Regiment Illinois Volunteer Infantry at Edgefield, Tennessee." Both Confederates and later Union forces were encamped on John Shelby's land by the Cumberland River. The railroad drawbridge, built in 1859 for use by the Edgefield & Kentucky and Louisville & Nashville railroads, has been replaced, but the original stone piers are still intact today. (Lithograph by Theodore Schrader, Chestnut Street, St. Louis, Missouri.) (TSLA.)

One

THE ESTATES

In 1870, the historian Charles Robert noted that East Nashville "Is one of the loveliest resident places in the South . . . and during the spring and hot summer months is a pleasant retreat for the businessman whose labors lie in Nashville." The Cumberland River served as a buffer from the old city, and the East End was known for being cooler in the summer and for having rich earth, abundant shade, and no foul slum.

The earliest settlers in East Nashville received 640-acre land grants from the State of North Carolina for fighting in the Revolutionary War. James Shaw sold his acreage to David Shelby in 1788. Shelby presented this land as a Christmas gift to his sons John and Anthony in 1818. John bought Anthony's share for $2,500 and built himself a home on what would now be Woodland Street (between Second and Third), which he called "Shelby Hall." In 1855, he built homes for his two daughters, Priscilla and Anna. He renamed these homes Fatherland and Boscobel.

Another 640-acre tract was given to Themy Purnell, who eventually sold it to William Hobson. Hobson's log home, built in 1807, still stands at 814 Woodland Street (wings were added and the log was covered with clapboard in 1826). Daniel Williams owned another tract and built a cabin in 1786 by the spring which would later be called "Lockeland." Gradually, cultivated land was sold off for large estates and country homes, which in turn were themselves subdivided. It appears that a number of prominent families began to sell their estates in East Nashville in the early part of the 20th century and move to the rapidly developing West End and Belle Meade areas. As East Nashville developed more, it lost much of its idyllic rural feel and there was money to be made selling building lots. Bishop McTyeire had planned to build Vanderbilt University in East Nashville, but was not able to acquire suitable land.

Vanderbilt University and the Tennessee Centennial Exposition turned public attention westward. The proliferation of industry also made some estates by the river less bucolic. Horace Greely Hill moved from his estate by the Cumberland in 1910 to Post Road, Percy Warner moved to Harding Road in 1912, and Johnson Bransford moved to Belle Meade in 1914.

MAP OF THE LOCKELAND NEIGHBORHOOD, 1908. The streets labeled Jones and Preist are now 17th Street. Lockeland, the J.B. Richardson estate, is seen at the top. Springside, the Lindsley estate, is at the bottom. Although Lockeland School and five houses replaced Lockeland, more than 20 lots were carved out of Springside. Both estates were razed and subdivided in the 1930s. (NR.)

ETCHING OF GENERAL BARROW'S HOUSE, 1860s. John Shelby built Boscobel for his daughter Anna, who married Washington Barrow. This home closely resembles Fatherland, so perhaps the etching was mislabeled. From "Map of Nashville and Edgefield, Davidson, Co. TN, 1860." Hayden & Booth, Civil Engineers & Surveyors. (TSLA.)

FATHERLAND IN THE 1890S. Designed by Adolphus Heiman and built by John Shelby in 1855, this home had double parlors, marble mantles, and a wrought iron spiral staircase to the cupola. Shelby, from which the street and park take their names, was a physician, state senator, and a postmaster of Nashville. He helped organize Nashville's first Jockey Club in 1816 and was a founder of Christ Episcopal Church in 1825. (NR.)

FATHERLAND, 701 SOUTH FIFTH STREET, 1952. Owned by Shelby's daughter, Mrs. John Phelan, after his death, Fatherland became the Florence Crittenton Home for Unwed Mothers in 1919. Still surrounded by 13 choice rolling acres by the river, the mansion and its gardens served this new role well until 1952, when it was acquired and demolished by the Nashville Housing Authority for an addition to the James Cayce Housing Development. (NR.)

THE DR. BENJAMIN F. WEAKLEY HOME, 1934. Built about 1849 on an estate totaling 100 acres, the home itself was located on what is now Sumner Avenue, near Eastland and Fourteenth Streets. Here Dr. Weakley and his wife, Mary Porter Weakley, reared their family of eight boys and two girls: Thomas Porter, Robert Weston, Oline, Mayline, Wickliffe, Franklin, William Harvey, Samuel D., James Harvey, and Mary. From this house the four boys of the family, who were of age when war flared between the states, marched away to join the Army of the Confederacy. After the war, they held prominent positions in business, education, and ministry in the Methodist Episcopal Church, South. The surrounding acreage gradually gave way to building lots, and the house itself was sold after the death of the last owner, Miss Mary E. Weakley, and replaced with four houses in 1935. (TSLA.)

GOVERNOR NEILL S. BROWN, 1885. The 14th and youngest governor of Tennessee, Brown served from 1848–1850. The only governor ever to live in East Nashville, Brown resided at an estate on Main Street called Idlewild. He is credited with naming the city of Edgefield. Brown was appointed United States Minister to Russia in 1850 and served in the State Constitutional Convention in 1870. (NR.)

931 MAIN STREET, 1955. Built by Lawrence Finn about 1855, this plantation home is a rare survivor on an otherwise densely developed corridor. It has been used for commercial purposes for more than 40 years. Besides this home, other antebellum estates found on the Gallatin Pike are: Renraw, Evergreen Place, Maplewood, the Halfway House, and Fairvue. (TSLA.)

LOCKELAND MANSION, 1914. Although an 1870 addition faced South Seventeenth Street on the site of the present Lockeland School, the original Federal-style house can be seen facing Woodland Street. Colonel Robert Weakley, a property surveyor, built the home in 1810 and named it for his wife, Jane, whose father was General Matthew Locke of North Carolina. Weakley County, where Robert Weakley was granted acreage for fighting in the Revolutionary War, is named for him. He was elected to the Constitutional Convention in 1787, served in the state legislature in 1796, and served in the state senate between 1799 and 1809. Weakley built Lockeland on the same land granted to Daniel Williams for fighting in the Revolutionary War. In 1786, Williams built a cabin on the site, the first structure built in this area, and stayed for ten years. Robert Weakley settled first by White's Creek when he came to Nashville in 1785. A farmer, politician, and businessman, he amassed several large tracts of land before his death on February 4, 1845 at the age of 81. (EBL.)

THE ORIGINAL FRONT OF THE HOUSE BUILT BY THE WEAKLEYS IN ABOUT 1810. The house was brick and the foundation was quarried stone. By the time this photograph was taken at the turn of the century, the entire house had been considerably altered and enlarged by a later owner who had added the mansard porch roof and new entrance. (LSNA.)

THE WEAKLEY FAMILY BURIAL VAULT, 1900. Weakley's children inherited and disposed of his estate. His son, Robert Locke Weakley, purchased the mansion and 398 adjoining acres. More land was sold off in later years, and the lot containing the tomb (1715 Forrest Avenue) was sold to a grandson, E.W. Hickman. In 1947, the remains were transferred to Mt. Olivet Cemetery, and the vault destroyed. (LSNA.)

THE REAR GALLERIES, 1900. Lockeland Mansion was L-shaped and had double galleries that faced the river. The grounds were very park-like and lush, and the galleries and yard were filled with ferns, potted palms, and urns planted with flowers. There was a vine-covered gazebo, and at different times through the years, there was a picket fence or a formal hedge between the front lawn and the sidewalk. (LSNA.)

THE FRONT OF LOCKELAND, 1900. Robert Locke Weakley died in 1848 without a will, and the Davidson County Chancery Court sold Lockeland at auction in July of 1849 to pay off his debts. Edwin Childress purchased the estate and 390 acres and sold it to his daughter and son-in-law, Mary Ann and Thomas Chadwell, for $1. The Chadwells remodeled the mansion with Second Empire-style porches and a tower. (TSLA.)

MR. JAMES B. RICHARDSON, 1900. A prominent businessman, Richardson purchased Lockeland and 8 acres in 1889. He discovered the curative powers of the Lockeland Spring and began to bottle the water. According to the writings of local historian Harry Gower, when the surrounding land sold off by the Chadwells was being developed in 1880, the name "Woodland Heights" was proposed, but Richardson suggested the name "Lockeland," and his motion was approved. (EBL.)

J.B. RICHARDSON'S DAUGHTER HENRIETTE, 1900. Although it is not clear exactly what the occasion is, her gown, hat, and elaborate bouquet are certainly the very height of fashion. Lockeland was her family's country home, and they lived downtown near the Capitol during the social season. (EBL.)

THE LOCKELAND TENNIS COURT, 1900. Henriette and her friends enjoy a game in what we would consider very formal attire. The tennis court was close to Holly Street, and the picket fence that ran the perimeter of the property can be seen in the background. (LSNA.)

DELIVERY WAGON FOR LOCKELAND SPRINGS WATER. After the ailing Richardson discovered that drinking the lithia spring water seemed to improve his health, he began to share it with friends. The fame of the water spread, and Richardson erected a bottling plant so that the health-giving water might be shared. (LSNA.)

THREE FRIENDS IN THE DOOR OF THE SPRING HOUSE. At the 1904 Louisiana Purchase Exposition in St. Louis, the Lockeland Spring water won a grand prize in recognition of its "unique mineral composition and salubrious quality." Advertisements claimed it was "one of the softest and purest waters yet discovered. A specific for diseases of kidneys, bladder, and stomach. A remedy for all forms of indigestion, dyspepsia, and rheumatic affections." (LSNA.)

WOMAN ON A BRIDGE IN FRONT OF THE LOCKELAND SPRING PROPERTY. The bottling plant can be seen in the background. In 1925, the 8 acres of adjacent land was sold and subdivided. The Lockeland Mansion was purchased by the city in 1939, razed, and Lockeland School built on the site. The Howe Bottling Company continued to distribute the spring water up until the 1940s. (LSNA.)

EDGEWOOD, 1890s. Edgewood was built by Colonel Anthony Wayne Johnson, a capitalist and friend of Andrew Jackson, James K. Polk, and Sam Houston. Johnson had extensive land holdings in East Nashville and had the mansion built in 1854 as he campaigned on horseback for the state senate. He served 1855–56 and retired the next year at 60. Although Johnson voted against secession in the spring of 1861, he supported his state when Tennessee left the Union. Despite the fact that he was born in New Hampshire, he held onto his Confederate convictions, and the conquering Yankees sent him to state prison and commandeered his house. Johnson was freed on April 25, 1863. After the war, his daughter Mary married Major John S. Bransford. Bransford was for many years vice-president of the Louisville and Nashville railroad. The Colonel gave Edgewood to the Bransfords around 1872, the year their son Johnson was born. (NR.)

THE ELIZABETH BRANSFORD-FRANCIS B. FOGG WEDDING PARTY. This wedding brought the union of two prominent Nashville families and estates. The groom was the son of Godfrey M. Fogg, a lawyer and president of Duck River Phosphate Company. The Fogg home was "Melrose" on the Nolensville Pike. This union was short-lived, as the Foggs divorced in 1901, but John Bransford purchased Melrose and it remained in the Bransford family for several years. (NR.)

EDGEWOOD, SEEN FROM WHERE NORTH 12TH STREET RUNS TODAY. Johnson and Annie Mary inherited Edgewood in 1907. Johnson's Bransford Realty Company was profitable selling suburban homes in East Nashville and the rapidly developing West End. In 1914, Bransford subdivided the acreage around Edgewood and sold the home place, eventually settling at Deerfield in Belle Meade. Edgewood lost its cupola in the 1933 tornado, but stood strong at 719 North 12th Street until 1962, when it was razed for an 18-unit apartment house. (TSLA.)

LYNNLAWN, EASTLAND AVENUE AND GALLATIN ROAD, ABOUT 1940. Built in 1845 by Thomas E. Stratton, this Italian Renaissance-style home was said to have been designed by William Strickland, the architect of the Tennessee Capitol. Sitting in a lawn of pecans, magnolias, and maples, the home took its name from the lynn trees which flanked the entryway. According to *History of Homes and Gardens of Tennessee*, Lynnlawn was commandeered during the Civil War by Prince Felix Salm-Salm, "son of the reigning Prince of Prussia and Brigadier-General of the northern army." The house had 18 rooms, with 17.5-foot frescoed ceilings on the first floor and 14.5-foot ceilings on the second. Lynnlawn was home to five generations of Strattons. In 1957, surrounded by commercial development, the home was sold by the last owner, Mrs. Edgar M. Foster, to the H.G. Hill Realty Company, who razed the mansion, but did not develop the property for 20 years, at which time they built a strip shopping center and supermarket. (TSLA.)

Mrs. Edgar M. Foster, 1940. Lynnlawn was opened to the public once in 1940 for the Garden Pilgrimage. The home was very well preserved, with its original furnishings, carpets, and a number of paintings by Ralph E.W. Earl. The 1824 portrait of the Ephraim H. Foster family, painted on bed ticking, was donated to the Fine Arts Center at Cheekwood by a Foster heir. (NR.)

The Back Gallery of Lynnlawn, 1940. The 4-acre grounds were extensively landscaped with brick bordered walks, formal beds, and a circular boxwood room. The site was surrounded by a lilac hedge, and the circular driveway was entered through a stone gate. (NR.)

The Entry Gate to Renraw on Gallatin Road. The lush grounds and long winding driveway can be seen where garages and parking lots for the Nashville Auto Diesel College are located today. (TSLA.)

A Formal Grouping of the Percy Warner Family in Front of Renraw (Warner Spelled Backward) about 1900. "Rufus" the crane is posed with the group. The occasion is not clear. (TSLA.)

RENRAW, ABOUT 1910. Zachariah Stull of Pennsylvania was given this property as a Revolutionary War land grant. Stull built a log house, and in 1855 built this house for his granddaughter, Mary Anne Childress. About 1886, the home was acquired by James C. Warner for a summer home. Warner, the son of a tailor, was one of the founders of the Tennessee Coal, Iron, and Railroad Company, which was a leading producer of coke and iron, and served as company president in the 1880s. He established the Warner Iron Company in 1880, and owned street railways and a textile mill. Upon James Warner's death in 1895, Renraw became the home of his son Percy, who developed the grounds of the estate. He sold Renraw about 1912 and moved to Royal Oaks on Harding Road in Belle Meade. (TSLA.)

A Vine-covered Pergola and a Gravel Walk Lined with Benches in the Renraw Garden. The gardens were a special concern of Mrs. James Warner, who grew "rare plants" in her greenhouse. (TSLA.)

Percy Warner, his Crane "Rufus," and Percy's Guest, Homer Davenport, a Cartoonist, in the Front Hall of Renraw. The gentleman in the center is Clare Lovett, an English gamekeeper employed by the Warners. Note the servants in the back hallway. (TSLA.)

PERCY WARNER WITH "RUFUS," THE CRANE. Warner built extensive aviaries at Renraw and had pheasants, cranes, peacocks, and other fowl. He had pheasants from Africa, India, Borneo, New Guinea, Sumatra, Java, China, Formosa, and Manchuria, and cranes from Africa, India, and Australia. Many of these birds were later given to Glendale Park. (TSLA.)

A WARNER CHILD, IN SOLDIER'S UNIFORM, ON THE PORCH OF THE PLAYHOUSE AT RENRAW. The Warner name would come to be associated with relaxation and beautiful scenery when Percy Warner's son-in-law, Luke Lea, and his brother Edwin donated funds to develop an extensive park southwest of the city. (TSLA.)

SPRINGSIDE, ABOUT 1895. Adrien V.S. Lindsley built Springside on one of the parcels sold off from Lockeland. Lindsley was the son of Philip Lindsley of the University of Nashville. The bulk of the property was subdivided in 1902, and Springside served as East End College for a few years. The remainder was subdivided in 1925, and the home razed in 1933. (EBL.)

SPRINGSIDE, ABOUT 1895. The house faced Holly Street, and the remnant of this driveway can still be seen today on North 15th Street. Lindsley opposed the secession of Tennessee in 1861, and because of his pro-Union loyalties, he often entertained officers. Twelve soldiers guarded his property for most of a year, and Springside was an unofficial headquarters for officers and the Cavalry Corps preparing for Hood's invasion in the winter of 1864. Lindsley was postmaster of Nashville during Reconstruction, from 1862–1867. Lindsley Park Drive is named for him. (EBL.)

Two

HOMES AND CHURCHES

East Nashville's separate identity is due in part to the Cumberland River separating it from the rest of the city, but also because it started out as separate municipalities. The city of Edgefield was incorporated in 1868 and was annexed as part of Nashville in 1883.

In his 1880 history of Nashville, W.W. Clayton said "Edgefield, being beautifully situated opposite Nashville upon a drift of glacial soil, with pure water and healthy country air, and united to the former by a fine wire bridge spanning the Cumberland naturally invited settlers and drew many of the businessmen and well-to-do families of Nashville to establish their homes there . . . schools sprang up, churches were built. Thus Edgefield became in a few years a beautiful, thriving, busy, suburban hamlet with a rapidly increasing population with the various institutions which constitute a refined and well-ordered community, and with her proportion of intelligent, progressive, and professional men."

Beginning in the 1880s, the Edgefield Land Company and others aggressively bought land for subdivision east of Edgefield's borders. The annexation of the suburb of Lockeland in 1905 and the opening of the Sparkman (Shelby) Street Bridge in 1909 fueled further development. An 1890 guidebook to Nashville says of East Nashville: "This flourishing and beautiful portion of Nashville was formerly known as Edgefield, and is to the city proper what Brooklyn is to New York; the place, par excellence, for the homes of many of the leading businessmen of the Rock City . . . It is well supplied with water, and it's laid out with a view to its becoming a large city in the near future, with wide streets at right angles, well macadamized, and lighted with gas . . . Three lines of street cars, under one management, run to all parts of the city, and the place is the most attractive portion of Nashville." An 1892 guidebook adds "this is the fashionable residence quarter . . . It has city water and lights, and all the conveniences afforded by location in the heart of the town." East Nashville still boasts a convenient location, with historic housing stock, beautiful churches, and elegant public buildings.

Beautiful Eastland

AT AUCTION

ON THE PREMISES

THURSDAY, MAY 8, 2:30 P. M.

70 HIGH-CLASS LOTS

We have positive instructions to subdivide and sell the 15 acres known as the WEAKLEY HOME PLACE. Bounded on the west by 14th street, east by 16th street. In two blocks of Woodland and Gallatin car, and one block of Woodland car on Eastland avenue. Surrounded by fine houses and high-class citizenship, situated in a beautiful grove, makes this one of the most desirable additions ever offered to the general public for home sites. Every lot must be sold regardless of price, as the sale is for division among the heirs. You are to make the price, and we will make the terms of one-fourth cash, balance in one, two and three years' time with interest. Do not fail to attend, as this is the accepted time to secure you a lot at your own price. Get off WOODLAND CAR at Eastland and 16th street for sale.

Conveyance at office to show the property. Do not forget time and place.

C. F. SHARPE & SONS,
W. S. ASHWORTH & CO. Agents

REAL ESTATE ADVERTISEMENT FROM *THE NASHVILLE AMERICAN*, APRIL 27, 1913. Although home ownership was less common before the FHA began to set standards for housing construction and insure long-term mortgage loans in the mid-1930s, the housing market was booming in Nashville early in the century. During this time, the old central city was being transformed from what we now call a "mixed use" district of homes and businesses to the center of business and commerce. Although some old homes downtown became boardinghouses for single persons, families were moving out to the new suburbs.

Horse-drawn Carriages in Edgefield in the 1890s (Possibly Russell Street), as It Appeared in *Art Work of Nashville*. The sidewalks are brick, but the road itself is still unpaved. Note the early streetlights and the mailbox. (NR.)

Russell Street, 1890s. The elaborate new Tulip Street Methodist Episcopal Church, which was just completed in 1892 in the fashionable Romanesque Revival style, can be seen on the left. (NR.)

JOHN FLETCHER CLENDENNING (HOLDING ANNE AMELIA), ANN FLETCHER CLENDENNING, AND NELL PARKER CLENDENNING. The group was photographed in 1906 in the front yard of their home at 916 Boscobel Street. During summers in the days before air conditioning, folks spent much time outdoors, as the man cooling himself on the porch and the girls playing hopscotch are doing. (TSLA.)

MRS. GRAINGER IN FRONT OF HER HOME AT 919 BOSCOBEL STREET IN THE 1890S. According to Amelia W. Edwards, a local historian, the house was painted white with gray trim. (TSLA.)

220 BOSCOBEL STREET, 1950S. This large old Italianate-style home would have been very close to business and industry by the 1950s. Many of these homes were razed as part of Urban Renewal and interstate construction.

HOME OF JUDGE HENRY COOPER, 209 SOUTH FIFTH STREET. Built in 1868–69 by A.G. Sanford, the soft red brick of this home has been painted yellow and the garden is enclosed by a wall.

RUSSELL STREET, 1890S, FROM ART WORK OF NASHVILLE. Although all of these stately homes survived the fire, only the one to the right (with the tower) survived Urban Renewal in the 1960s. It now has a large garden where the other homes stood. (NR.)

FATHERLAND STREET IN THE 1930S. By this time, the West End had surpassed Edgefield in popularity, but the area was still solidly middle class, as this gentleman in the snazzy car could attest. (HEI.)

ANOTHER VIEW OF FATHERLAND STREET IN THE 1930S. The well-dressed couple is not identified, but the houses are numbers 929 and 931. Note the two men in jacket and tie lounging on the lawn. (HEI.)

J.B. Richardson Engine Co. No. 14, Affectionately Known as the "Holly Street Firehall," 1915. Neighbors organized the Lockeland Improvement League and lobbied to get one of the two firehalls scheduled to be built in the suburbs. (TSLA.)

The Holly Street Firehall, 1916. The firehall opened with formal ceremonies on October 1, 1914, and was named in honor of J.B. Richardson, who owned the Lockeland Mansion. Richardson, a philanthropist who had served as president of the United Charities of Nashville, died the previous year ,and naming the station after him was a way for the city to honor him. (TSLA.)

AND HOLLY STREETS ——— NASHVILLE, TENN.
1917

HOLLY STREET FIREHALL, 1917. Note the lush cannas, vines, and potted palms. A small birdcage hangs in the portico. The firehall was designed by Nashville's first city architect, James B. Yeaman, and was designed to blend in with the residential neighborhood. It was the first firehall in the city built specifically for motorized fire trucks. The adjacent 0.2-acre lot was purchased by East Nashville citizens and presented to the city on December 12, 1921 as a public park and playground. The park was named for Fire Chief Herman Bass, and the firemen maintained the flower beds and supervised the playground. The neighbors did not want the lot developed, because having it open gave a better view of the beautiful firehall and guaranteed that the firemen would not be disturbed. When the city proposed closing the firehall in the early 1980s, residents successfully petitioned to keep it open and raised funds for its restoration. (TSLA.)

CHILDREN ON THE SIDEWALK AT SOUTH SEVENTEENTH STREET, IN FRONT OF THE LOCKELAND MANSION, ABOUT 1905. The two boys in long pants to the left, one black and one white, appear to be pulling the younger children in shorts. (LSNA.)

THE JESSE HITT RESIDENCE, NORTHWEST CORNER OF 16TH AND FATHERLAND, 1914. This appears to have been a substantial home. It is no longer standing, and the lot is empty, but used as a side yard for another residence. (TSLA.)

THE TEN-ROOM RESIDENCE OF MR. STONE ON CHADWELL AVENUE (HOLLY STREET), 1914.
This photograph is interesting because it shows the fine line between suburban and rural life in
the early part of the century. A large barn and smaller outbuildings in the distance can be
seen. The side yard has been developed, and Shelby Golfcourse is on the other side. (TSLA.)

A COUPLE ON THE FENCE STAIR ON THE LOCKELAND ESTATE. A number of pastures and
meadows still existed in East Nashville early in the century. There were fences around the Rose
Bank Dairy Farm on Eastland Avenue. Fencing surrounded the Lockeland estate lands and
water bottling operations, and pastures ran along Sixteenth Street and at the "East End" of the
city near Fourteenth Street. (LSNA.)

LILLIAN STREET, 1914. This part of the Lockeland neighborhood seems a little more rural because there are not sidewalks or streetcar lines, although a line eventually ran down Nineteenth Street. When Lockeland School was located on Lillian, students would play in the dusty Eighteenth Street, except when it was muddy. (TSLA.)

NELLIE MCDOUGAL, IN APRON AND DUST CAP, AND CHICKENS IN THE BACKYARD OF HER HOME AT 1228 CHAPEL AVENUE, 1918. Chicken coops, garden houses, small garages, and servant houses (on certain streets) were common in the small backyards. (TSLA.)

1624 HOLLY STREET, AROUND 1918. Picket fencing or hedges around front yards and plank or wire fencing around backyards seems to have been popular. Note the double swing in the side yard. The side lot now has a small house on it. (MNA.)

MRS. BRANSFORD'S RESIDENCE, SOUTHEAST CHADWELL (HOLLY) AND SEVENTEENTH STREET, 1914. This home was built by Mary Chadwell Priest and Thomas Priest. Mr. Priest was a prominent lawyer and one-time attorney general. In 1902, the Priest homeplace was broken up into more than one hundred lots. The home looks very much today as it did almost 85 years ago. (TSLA.)

41

FATHERLAND STREET, 1914. The dome of the Seventeenth Street Christian Church can be seen in the far right. One of the streetcar lines was the Fatherland line, and although many of the houses had driveways during this period, it does not appear that many cars were on the road. (TSLA.)

TAYLOR MILTON WRIGHT, IN MILITARY UNIFORM, AND FRIEND, BY 1700 SHELBY AVENUE, ABOUT 1918. The ground is covered with snow. (TSLA.)

This American foursquare on the corner of Gartland Avenue and Twelfth Street was built by the Woodland Presbyterian Church and used as its manse from 1917–1948, when a newer house was purchased. (Woodland Presbyterian Church.)

HILARY HOWSE, MAYOR OF NASHVILLE FROM 1909–1915 AND AGAIN FROM 1923–1938. Howse made his reputation as an opponent of Prohibition and as a social reformer. The charming mayor lived at 607 North Fourteenth Street and had a summer house in Haysboro, a resort community in what is now North Inglewood and the National Cemetery section of Madison. (TSLA.)

THE EAST BRANCH CARNEGIE LIBRARY, 1950s. Designed by New York architect Albert Randolph Ross, who designed a number of Carnegie libraries, the East Branch was built in 1919 with a $25,000 gift from Andrew Carnegie. As Carnegie required, the city provided land and utilities and the residents raised funds for sidewalks and landscaping. Modern signage and lampposts added in 1962 were recently removed, and there are plans to restore the interior. The North Branch Carnegie and the East Branch Carnegie are the only two libraries built with funds from the philanthropist left in Nashville. The 1904 Carnegie Library at Eighth and Union was razed about 1965 and the Ben West Library built on the site. (MNA.)

A Birthday Party for the Librarian, May 8, 1934. From left to right are: Mr. Stratton Foster, Mrs. Walter L. Jones, Mr. Charles C. Trabue, Mrs. Lillian B. Fleming, Mr. Joe Boyd, Dr. A.S. Allen, Mr. F.K. W. Drury, Mr. J.J. Keyes, Mrs. Y.W. Haley, and Mr. George H. Cate. (NR.)

The Old Bell Residence, Next Door to Woodland Presbyterian Church. The building was used by that congregation as a fellowship hall for a number of years. In 1957, the residence was torn down, and their Centennial Wing was built on the site. (Woodland Presbyterian Church.)

THE DIXIE TABERNACLE, A RELIGIOUS REVIVAL HOUSE AT 410 FATHERLAND STREET. The Tabernacle was home to the Grand Ole Opry from 1936 to 1939. The Tabernacle seated two thousand on crude benches and had rehearsal rooms, a radio control room, and a well-lighted stage. The Opry moved to the War Memorial Auditorium in 1939 and to the Ryman Auditorium in 1943. (TSLA.)

GRAND OLE OPRY PERFORMANCE. During the Opry's days at the Dixie, a number of stars stayed at Mom Upchurch's Boardinghouse at 620 Boscobel Street, including the Carter Family, Grandpa Jones, Stonewall Jackson, and Carl Smith. The boardinghouse was operated by Delia Upchurch, in an old stone house that is still on Boscobel today. (TSLA.)

THE SHELBY AVENUE BRIDGE, 1909.
The Shelby Avenue Bridge was
constructed in 1909 as a way for city
reformers to clean up a slum on the south
side of Broadway called Black Bottom.
The bridge takes its name from the street
on the east side and has served as another
vital link between East Nashville and
downtown. (TSLA.)

Officers of the Blind Girls' Home

THE BLIND GIRLS' HOME, 1918. The Blind Girls' Home was constructed in 1903 by the State of Tennessee. The "Fear Not Circle" of the Kings Daughters and Sons, an organization devoted to Christian activities, operated the home from 1903 to 1980. They held linen showers, lawn parties in the summer, and a Christmas bazaar to raise funds. The building was rehabilitated as an apartment house in 1982. (NR.)

EDGEFIELD BAPTIST CHURCH, 700 RUSSELL STREET, AROUND 1895. Philanthropist Andrew Carnegie paid for half of the cost of the Moller organ, which was installed in 1908. This is one of the grand old churches to survive the 1916 fire. (TSLA.)

NORTH EDGEFIELD BAPTIST CHURCH, 1900. Established in 1887 as a mission church by some members of Edgefield Baptist, notably H.W. Buttorff and John D. Anderson, this beautiful building is no longer standing. (TSLA.)

LOCKELAND BAPTIST CHURCH, SIXTEENTH AND HOLLY STREETS, 1914. This 1903 section of the church, built on land given by Colonel W.M. Woodcock, can still be seen on Sixteenth Street behind the sanctuary built in 1929. (TSLA.)

EAST END UNITED METHODIST CHURCH, ABOUT 1915. East End was organized with 16 members in November of 1889, and the first building was a frame structure at 1100 Fatherland Street. By 1905, the congregation numbered four hundred and had outgrown the Fatherland Street building. Construction on the present church building, at what was the east end of the city, began in October of 1905. The church cost $14,000, and the cornerstone was laid on Sunday, October 27, 1907. The sanctuary was built in 1910, and Andrew Carnegie paid half the cost of the organ. The signs in this photograph read: "East End Men Want You, 9:30, Come." (East End UMC.)

TULIP STREET UNITED METHODIST CHURCH, ABOUT 1900. Designed by T.L. Dismukes and completed by J.E. Woodward, this imposing Richardsonian Romanesque structure was completed in 1892. Carillon chimes from the Tennessee Centennial Exposition were purchased and installed in the taller tower in 1897. (HEI.)

FIRST EDGEFIELD PRESBYTERIAN CHURCH, ABOUT 1870. Services were held in a schoolhouse on Fourth and Fatherland Streets until this building was completed. It was dedicated free-of-debt on April 3, 1859 and used until a new building was erected in 1887. (TSLA.)

WOODLAND STREET PRESBYTERIAN CHURCH, 1916. Built in 1887 as the First Edgefield Presbyterian Church, the name was changed to Woodland Street Presbyterian Church in 1889 because Edgefield was no longer a separate city, and it was confusing to have two "first" churches. It is seen here immediately after the 1916 fire. (NR.)

FIRST CHURCH OF THE NAZARENE, 510 WOODLAND STREET, 1940S. The Nazarene Church was founded as part of the Holiness Movement by J.O. McClurkan and others and met in the old Tulip Street Methodist Church. They purchased and rebuilt the burned-out Woodland Street Presbyterian Church in 1916 and used it until they built a new sanctuary in 1950. (FCN.)

SEVENTEENTH STREET CHURCH OF CHRIST, 1914. Built in 1908, the church was later known as Seventeenth Street Christian Church, and then Lockeland Christian Church. A fire in the late 1950s resulted in the loss of the beautiful stained-glass windows. The congregation disbanded in 1983, and the neighborhood association kept the building from being razed. (TSLA.)

53

WOODLAND PRESBYTERIAN CHURCH, 1917. After the March 22, 1916 fire in Edgefield, this congregation sold their burned building to the Pentecostal Church of the Nazarene congregation and purchased land at Eleventh and Gartland Avenue. Designed by noted architect C.K. Colley, the imposing Neoclassical structure was dedicated on November 10, 1918. (Woodland Presbyterian Church.)

MR. PALMER'S SUNDAY SCHOOL CLASS AT WOODLAND PRESBYTERIAN CHURCH, EASTER SUNDAY, APRIL 1948. Woodland's membership peaked at approximately six hundred around this time. There are certainly an interesting variety of hats pictured. (Woodland Presbyterian Church.)

ST. JOHN THE EVANGELIST CHURCH, 1860s. This is the only surviving photograph of the church. Many Catholics migrated south to work on the railroads, and since three railroads terminated in Edgefield, there was a sizable Catholic population. This church was dedicated in 1857 and replaced in 1871. (Holy Name Catholic Church.)

ST. COLUMBA CHURCH, RECTORY, AND SCHOOL, 1880s. St. Columba was built to replace St. John the Evangelist, and stood on the south side of Main Street. The Little Sisters of the Poor had a convent and home for the aged across the street. The church and convent burned in the 1916 fire. The home moved to Horton Avenue, and the church was replaced with Holy Name Catholic Church. (Holy Name Catholic Church.)

ST. ANN'S EPISCOPAL CHURCH, 1890. The cornerstone was laid in 1882, and the church was consecrated on June 10, 1885. The church had been organized in a schoolhouse on Fatherland Street in 1858. (St. Ann's Episcopal Church.)

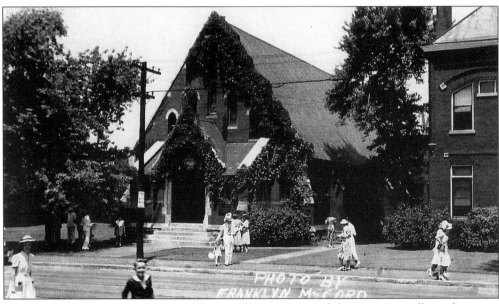

ST. ANN'S EPISCOPAL, 1940S. Note the steeple is missing and the rectory is still standing next to the church. The rectory was razed in the late 1950s for the construction of the Howe Wing. (St. Ann's Episcopal Church.)

SAINT ANN'S EPISCOPAL CHURCH, 1958. This photograph was taken during the groundbreaking for the Harry Howe Wing. The Howe family donated much of the cost for the wing. Mrs. Harry Howe, the older woman in the hat, is in the center. Corra Howe is remembered for her garden, called "Wildings" which surrounded her home on Greenwood Avenue. The garden featured about three hundred varieties of flowering trees, shrubs, and plants, many native to Tennessee. After her death, her gardens were transplanted to the Tennessee Botanical Gardens at Cheekwood. (St. Ann's Episcopal Church.)

EASTLAND CHURCH OF CHRIST, "THE CHURCH BUILT IN A DAY." The day was Thanksgiving Day, 1910. At 9:30 a.m. the framing is done and the clapboard is being installed. (Eastwood Christian.)

EASTLAND CHURCH, LATER IN THE DAY OF ITS CONSTRUCTION. By 11:30 a.m., finish carpentry is being done, rafters are up, and decking is being nailed down. (Eastwood Christian.)

3:30 P.M. The windows are in, the building is being painted, and the roof is being finished. (Eastwood Christian.)

4:30 P.M. The job is complete and workers have neckties, vests, and jackets back on to pose for this photograph. It was the union of Eastland Christian and Woodland Christian that formed the present congregation known as Eastwood Christian Church. (Eastwood Christian.)

EASTWOOD CHRISTIAN CHURCH, 1949. Eastwood Christian Church was formed from the merger of two earlier congregations, Woodland Christian and Eastland Christian. Ground is being broken for the construction of the sanctuary. Note the houses across Eastland Avenue. (ECC.)

THE EDUCATION BUILDING FOR EASTWOOD. This building was constructed in 1933 and was designed by the firm of Marr & Holman. The sanctuary was completed in 1950, according to plans drawn in 1933. (ECC.)

Three

SCHOOLS

Late in the 19th century, East Nashville was home to several prestigious female academies. In Morrison's *City of Nashville* guidebook (1892), Boscobel College is described: "Boscobel College for Young Ladies, situated in a beautiful and retired part of the suburbs, near the electric railway, one mile from the center of the city, has for its aim the higher education of the daughters of our land, so as to place them on a plane of equality in the world, as respects their mental equipment and resources for a livelihood, with the young men growing up beside them . . . It is a boarding and day school, having over one hundred pupils, members of the best families of this and adjacent states. Ten acres of woodland, native forest trees, surround the college building, affording delightful shade through the warmer months, and ample room, for exercise, so necessary to mental and physical development. Free from the noise, dust, and confusion of the crowded thoroughfares; crowning one of the highest elevations about the city; supplied with every modern convenience for the comfort, health, and happiness of the pupil." Trevecca College, the first school opened by the Church of the Nazarene denomination, also had a long presence in East Nashville, settling in the Warner estate, Renraw, in about 1918. In the early 1930s, they held classes in homes on Woodland Street. The Nashville Auto Diesel College occupies Renraw today.

Neighborhood schools have also been important to this community of strong neighborhoods. Warner School was the first school in Nashville to house special education classes. Former Warner principal R.N. Chenault also began the first primary unit in Tennessee here. East High School was one of the first suburban high schools built in the city and graduated a number of notable Nashvillians, mayors and politicians, entertainers, and leaders in business and civic organizations. Today, East Nashville retains some of the most historic and beautiful school buildings in the city.

WARNER SCHOOL, SECOND GRADE, 1897. Miss Lena Wilson, far right, was the teacher. (NR.)

BOSCOBEL COLLEGE, 1908. Boscobel means "beautiful grove," and Boscobel College occupied 10 acres of woodland. The college was built around the mansion owned by Shelby Williams. This was the same name given by John Shelby to the home he built for his daughter Anna. Priscilla Shelby's first husband was David Williams, and it is unclear whether or not Shelby Williams was related to the Shelby family. (NR.)

BOSCOBEL COLLEGE, 1890S. The mansion, at the center of the campus, was built of handmade blue-burned brick and had marble mantles imported from Italy. Boscobel College was razed in the 1940s, along with 40 other structures on Boscobel Heights, to make way for the James Cayce Housing Development. (NR.)

GRADUATES OF BOSCOBEL COLLEGE, 1898. Boscobel College had over one hundred pupils. It advertised its "literary faculty" and "music and art advantages unsurpassed," and promised to prepare the young ladies "for life's work and its duties." (TSLA.)

AN AD FOR MRS. M.E. CLARK'S SELECT SCHOOL FOR YOUNG LADIES. This boarding school, which accommodated 50 students, was founded by Mrs. Clark in 1885. The four-story house was situated on 14 acres. Instruction was given by the "best scholars" Mrs. Clark could secure, and she was known to travel in Europe to investigate new methods of education. (MNA.)

631 WOODLAND STREET, ABOUT 1961. Henri Weber conducted Edgefield Female Academy here from 1868 to 1879. Another school, East End College for Young Ladies, operated in the Springside mansion farther down Woodland Street from 1890 to 1905. (NR.)

THE OLD MEIGS SCHOOL, 1890S, FROM *ART WORK OF NASHVILLE*. Built in 1883 to the same plans as Pearl School, Meigs was the first high school for African Americans in Nashville. The high school department was transferred to Pearl in 1897. A small African-American population was attracted to East Nashville by jobs in the lumber mills and factories by the river. These African Americans settled north of Main Street. (NR.)

EASTLAND SCHOOL, 1905. Eastland School was at Chapel and Douglas Avenue until the 1950s, Gothic-inspired architecture was popular for educational buildings early in the century. (MBE.)

ST. COLUMBA SCHOOL, 1880S. In 1878, The old St. John's Church was converted into a school for St. Columba Church. This building burned in 1881 and was replaced with a new building in 1883. The Dominican Sisters returned to teach that same year. (Holy Name Catholic Church.)

ST. COLUMBA SCHOOL, DECEMBER 6, 1914. Fashions appear to have changed quite a bit between the 1880s and the early 20th century. St. Columba School burned in 1916 and was replaced with Holy Name School. (Holy Name Catholic Church.)

HOLY NAME SCHOOL, 1929. From left to right are: (front row) Jo Ann Floursh, Mary Francis Shorenburger, and Edna Wehby; (back row) Adelea Corcoran, Sister Carmelitta, and Margaret Tallman. (TSLA.)

HOLY NAME SCHOOL, GRADUATING CLASS, 1929. From left to right are: (front row) Wehby, Shorenburger, Tallman, Corcoran, Flourish, and Sister Carmelitta; (third row) Hofstetter, Wilk, Monsignor Hardeman, Wiggers, and Varallo; (back row) Clarke, Sanders, Petrucelli, and Bohan. (TSLA.)

TREVECCA COLLEGE, 1925. Trevecca College moved to the old Percy Warner estate, Renraw, in 1918. A residence hall has been added beside the old mansion. Streets named Trevecca and McClurkan are reminders today of Trevecca's presence at the site. (TNUA.)

A FLIER ADVERTISING TREVECCA COLLEGE, 1920S. "In the 'Athens of the South' in one of the best residential sections of the city, on the Gallatin-Inglewood car line . . . Large, beautiful shaded campus, one of the most desirable college sites in all this beautiful southland." (TNUA.)

TREVECCA STUDENTS, 1929. Because of the Great Depression, the school had financial problems in the early 1930s and moved to Woodland Street, holding classes in both the Nazarene church building and homes. In the mid-1930s, the school built a new campus on Murfreesboro Road. (TNUA.)

THE ORIGINAL WARNER SCHOOL, 1890s. Warner School was opened in 1894 and was described at the time as "the largest and most imposing structure on the east side of the river" and "a monument to [the city's] liberality and progressive spirit." (TSLA.)

WARNER SCHOOL, 1915. The clock tower had been removed and the building somewhat simplified. Named for James C. Warner, a member of the Edgefield Board of Education, this building burned in the 1916 fire. (NR.)

WARNER SCHOOL, 1918. This building replaced the one lost in the fire. Classes were held at various other buildings in Edgefield until the school, which cost $152,000, was complete. Notice the urns which mark the entrance to the formal gardens of East Park, also built in the aftermath of the fire. (TSLA.)

WARNER ADDITION, 1949. A west wing with nine classrooms and a cafeteria was added to Warner School in 1949. Earlier in the decade (1941) a fire destroyed the roof and top floor, and school superintendent W.A. Bass had to file with the War Production Board to release materials to rebuild the school. (MNA.)

THE ORIGINAL LOCKELAND SCHOOL, EIGHTEENTH AND LILLIAN STREETS, 1908. Lockeland School was built in 1898. Before this, the only county school in the 18th district was Spout Spring School at 1818 Vaughn Pike (Eastland Avenue). Lockeland had a large center hall where coats and hats were hung, with classrooms on both sides. Straight back was a large study hall with a coal stove in the center and a platform and blackboard at the end. Girls sat on the west side of the aisle and boys on the east. (TSLA.)

THE OLD LOCKELAND SCHOOL, 1950. After the new Lockeland School was built in 1939, the old school was used for an annex for the first and second grades. By the time this photograph was taken, it was an annex for Warner School, and in 1966, it was razed and three houses built on the site. (MNA.)

LOCKELAND SCHOOL, 1951. Lockeland School was built in 1939 on the site of the Lockeland Mansion and was designed by the architect C.K. Colley. Harry Gower, a local historian who wrote in the 1970s of his experiences growing up in Lockeland, relates that when he told Mr. Colley he lived near this site, the architect said to him, "I will plan the prettiest school in the city for you." (MNA.)

LOCKELAND SCHOOL, SIDE VIEW, 1951. Two additions have been necessary to Lockeland School since it was built, and not long after the building was complete, the Lockeland Men's Club lobbied the city to fill the back of the schoolyard to make it level for children to play. Plans are underway to create an interpretive mini-park near the historic Lockeland Spring. (MNA.)

M.M. Ross School, 1930s. At the time Ross School was constructed, Ordway Place was known as Grove Avenue. The high stone basement, arched entrance, and rusticated quoins give this building an urban, imposing look we are somewhat unaccustomed to for school buildings. (NR.)

M.M. Ross School, Eighth Grade, 1937. Ross School was in continuous use as an elementary school until 1986, when a new school was constructed behind East Middle School. Today it is still being used as a Head Start Center. (NR.)

EAST HIGH SCHOOL, 1932. East opened to 1,500 students in grades nine through 12 in the fall of 1932. At the time, the city was embarking on a plan to provide neighborhood high schools for all parts of the city. (MNA.)

EAST NASHVILLE JR. HIGH SCHOOL, *NASHVILLE BANNER*, 1936. East Junior High, designed by George D. Waller, was constructed through the Public Works Administration, a Depression-era program created to boost the economy by providing work for private companies. The Works Progress Administration created jobs for the unemployed. (NR.)

THE EAST HIGH LIBRARY, 1933. Designed by the firm Marr & Holman, who also designed the State Supreme Court building and old downtown post office, East was one of the finest and best equipped schools in the state when it opened. (MNA.)

EAST NASHVILLE JUNIOR HIGH FACULTY, 1937. Both East High and East Junior High were fortunate to have excellent teachers and administrators from the very beginning. (NR.)

EAST HIGH RIFLE TEAM, 1947. From left to right are: (front row) Sgt. Oscar Carver, Sgt. Milton Cutrell, Cpl. Alvin Willis, Tech. Sgt. John Blazer, and First Lt. Hoyt Eakes; (back row) Principal William Henry Oliver, Lt. Col. Elmer Todd, Capt. Clarence Bomar, First Lt. Leonard DeLaney, Cpl. Enrico Pruter, Sgt. Charles Covington, T-3 Alton McConnell (manager), and Master Sgt. Roy O'Kane (ROTC instructor). (MNA.)

EAST HIGH CHEERLEADERS, 1945. East had much to cheer about through the years, both on and off the field. Leadership on the field was given by Jimmy Armistead, East's physical education director and first head coach, and later by Watson Magee, C.V. Baker, Fred "Ox" McKibbon, Tommy Owen, Hilary Martin, Vic Varallo, and others. (MNA.)

EAST HIGH WITH CLOCK TOWER, 1946. East's Memorial Clock Tower was installed after the Second World War in honor of the 59 alumni who died in that conflict. (MNA.)

THE MALONE HOUSE, 1951. Everett "E.B." Malone was the longtime custodian of East and moved into this building in 1937. On 1920 fire insurance maps of the area, a post office is shown across the street from a large Victorian-style house on the East site. This building resembles the post office and could have been part of a civic grouping popular during the City Beautiful Movement. (MNA.)

THE J.J. KEYES STADIUM, 1933. Only the city's second football stadium, Keyes Stadium was named after East's first principal. The scoreboard and some fencing blew away in the 1933 tornado, but the stadium served the school well long afterwards. It was torn down in 1987 to create room for a new Ross Elementary School. (MNA.)

WILLIAM HENRY OLIVER, 1935. William Henry Oliver was the beloved principal of East from 1939–1957, when he was elected superintendent of schools. As superintendent, Oliver had the difficult task of helping to develop a school desegregation plan that was later used as a model nationally. Students continued to send correspondence to his Eastland Avenue home until his death in 1991. (MNA.)

ENTRANCE TO EAST HIGH SCHOOL, 1961. East operated as a high school until 1986, when it was closed and reopened as a middle school. It currently serves also as a literature magnet school. (MNA.)

EAST HIGH GRADUATION, 1961. Mayor Ben West is at the microphone with Principal Robert G. Neil. East continues to have an extremely loyal and active alumni association. During its long history, it graduated Mayor Richard Fulton, Mayor Bill Boner, Oprah Winfrey, Ralph Emery, and other well-known Nashvillians. (MNA.)

Four
TRYING TIMES

Over the years, East Nashville has had more than its share of trying times. One of the most devastating events in Nashville's history has come to be known as the "East Nashville Fire." On Wednesday, March 22, 1916, a fire broke out in the rear of Seagraves Planing Mill, and was swept east by 44- to 51-mile per hour gales. A total of 648 buildings were burned, one life was lost, and three thousand were left homeless. A similar natural disaster 17 years later hit East Nashville particularly hard. On March 14, 1933 a tornado whipped across Tennessee. The twister was 200 feet off the ground in West Nashville, dropped low enough to rip the tops off some brick buildings downtown, and then jumped the river and did its heaviest damage. Second and Woodland were hit hardest, but the storm fanned out across Gallatin Road from Eastland to Inglewood. Ten residents were left dead and hundreds injured. Furniture littered Shelby Park, and blocks of houses were ruined. Although other parts of the state received more damage, this disaster too is referred to as the "East Nashville Tornado." Floods in the winter of 1926–27 were the worst in the city's history. The Cumberland River overflowed its banks on Christmas Day, 1926, and five thousand people were forced to evacuate their homes. Other "trying times" are more recent. In the early 1960s, as highway construction and the booming post-war economy encouraged a general flight to the suburbs, federal money for "Urban Renewal" often did more harm than good, but through it all, East Nashville has persevered.

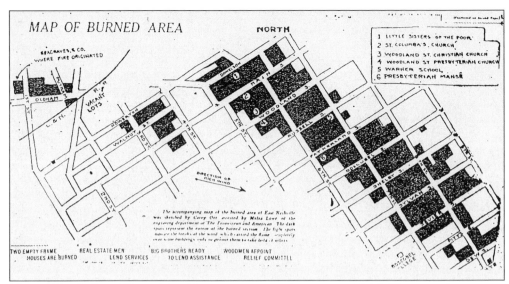

MAP OF FIRE'S PATH FROM *THE TENNESSEAN AND AMERICAN*, 1916. The most damage was between Donelson and Dew Street, 5th and 9th. (NR.)

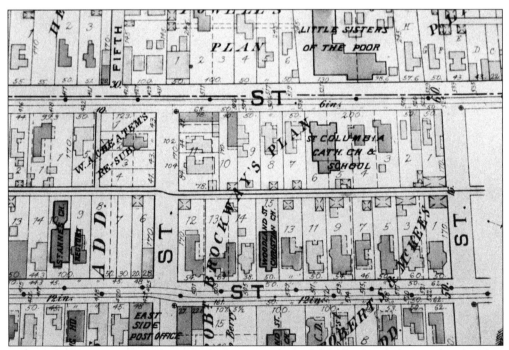

MAP OF EDGEFIELD, 1908. This map shows many of Edgefield's landmarks lost in the 1916 fire, including the Little Sisters of the Poor Convent and St. Columba Catholic Church and School on Main Street and Woodland Street Christian Church and Woodland Street Presbyterian Church on Woodland Street. St. Ann's Episcopal Church is middle left. (NR.)

82

EAST NASHVILLE FIRE, MARCH 22, 1916. People walk the streets through the devastation. Notice the picket fences still standing where the houses are gone. (TSLA.)

EAST NASHVILLE FIRE, MARCH 22, 1916. A total of 648 buildings were burned in this fire and three thousand people were left homeless. (TSLA.)

EAST NASHVILLE FIRE, MARCH 22, 1916. Notice Edgefield Baptist Church, a rare survivor. This photograph might have been taken from the tower of Tulip Street Methodist. (TSLA.)

EAST NASHVILLE FIRE, MARCH 22, 1916. The house, middle right, still stands on Fatherland Street and is one of the oldest houses in Edgefield. (TSLA.)

EAST NASHVILLE FIRE, 1916. The magnitude of the task of cleaning up after the fire can be better appreciated after viewing the stacks and stacks of bricks. The tower of Tulip Street Methodist can be seen in the distance. (MPD.)

EAST NASHVILLE FIRE, 1916. This photograph was taken from the corner of Woodland and South Sixth Street. Some chimneys are still standing, but these lots are being cleared for East Park. (MPD.)

THE EAST BANK DURING FLOOD, WINTER 1926–27. The Cumberland River overflowed its banks on Christmas Day, 1926, and five thousand people had to evacuate their homes. (NR.)

SHELBY PARK, 1927. Floods in the winter of 1926–1927 were the worst in the city's history. Here, the bulk of Shelby Park is completely under water. The railroad trestle is seen in the distance. (MPD.)

EASTLAND AVENUE, 1933. Although sports writer Grantland Rice grew up on Woodland Street, his grandparents lived on Eastland Avenue. After their home was destroyed by the 1933 tornado, Eastwood Christian Church built an education building on the site. (Eastwood Christian.)

EASTLAND AVENUE, 1933. Every house within five blocks of Sixteenth Street and Eastland Avenue was damaged. Riverside Drive also suffered extensive damage. (Eastwood Christian.)

MAYOR BEN WEST AND MEMBERS OF THE CITY COUNCIL. Mayor West is unveiling plans for the East Nashville Urban Renewal Project of 1958. Designed to revitalize the area, the East Nashville Urban Renewal Project called for a "broad new boulevard" (Spring Street), a 40-acre boat marina, and "wide industrial, residential, parks, schools, and facilities improvement." The marina was not included in the final plan, but houses were cleared to double the size of East Park. Douglas Park and many new businesses were built on Main Street, and a number of new roads were completed. An estimated 1,287 structures were cleared in the first phase of the project, and an entire street (Tenth) was cleared and rebuilt as part of the Shelby Heights Project. (MNA.)

RUSSEL STREET, 1961. This home at the corner of Russell and Eighth Streets is being cleared as part of Urban Renewal in May 1961. The windows have already been removed. Although the project stressed the importance of improved housing, many of the lots cleared stayed vacant for 25 years. (TSLA.)

FATHERLAND STREET, 1954. This home on the northwest corner of Fatherland and Fifth Streets, which had belonged to Shade Murray early in the century, was razed in July of 1963. (TSLA.)

PLAN FOR "BOSCOBEL HEIGHTS," MARR & HOLMAN, ARCHITECTS, 1940. "Boscobel Heights" was an early renewal project, as 40 structures were cleared to build this public housing development. During this period, public housing was being built to Garden City ideals, that is in clusters surrounded by green space and playgrounds. James Cayce, chairman of the Nashville Housing Authority Board, died while the project was being completed, and the development was instead named in honor of him. (TSLA.)

SAM LEVY HOMES, EARLY 1950S. At the time that these housing projects were built, they were considered nice apartments. They were built in a ring around the city of Nashville to act as a "buffer" between residential neighborhoods and the urban and industrial parts of the city center. (MNA.)

Five

BUSINESSES

East Nashville remained mostly residential, except for the area along the river and the railroad tracks, until the 1930s, although a number of lumber mills, furniture manufacturing operations, and other manufacturing concerns settled at the river late in the 19th century. Farther into East Nashville, commercial development follows the pattern found in similar late 19th and early 20th-century neighborhoods. Commercial enterprises are found on street corners throughout the residential parts of the area, because the community developed during the days of the "walking city," when ice-boxes were in use and frequent trips to the corner market were necessary. In the 1920s, many retail concerns grew up in the formerly residential area we now know as Five Points, along Woodland Street, and the bungalows on Main Street also gradually gave way to businesses during the 1930s and 1940s.

Many of the corner stores, like Simpkins Grocery on Shelby Avenue, or pharmacies like Hoosers on Woodland or Eastside on Fatherland, operated up until the 1970s and 1980s. Former residents still have fond memories of Sandersons, which later became Fulton Five & Ten on Woodland, Powell Phillips' Esso Service Station, Mrs. Ashbough's Candy Shop, Vester's Billiards, and the Woodland Theater. East Nashville continues to be a walking community where the groceries, the post office, and the hardware store are all close by and new restaurants and shops are once again opening on the area's historic commercial corners. Although planners may tout "the new urbanism," East Nashvillians have been enjoying "the old urbanism" all along.

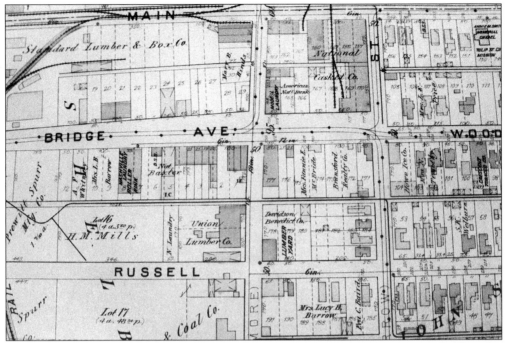

MAP OF EDGEFIELD, 1908. Bridge Avenue became Woodland at Barrow (2nd). This intersection is pictured on page 94. Notice the lumber companies by the river.

MAP OF FIVE POINTS, 1908. Main Street is to the left and Woodland to the right (trolley route marked). Lindsley Street is now called Clearview. Houses can be seen along Woodland where businesses are today. Most of the storefronts in Five Points were built in the 1920s. The only commercial building pictured is the Cumberland Telephone & Telegraph Walnut Exchange Building (now the Hot Rod Shop).

WOODLAND STREET BRIDGE, 1890S. Industry developed on the East Bank late in the 19th century. This suspension bridge was built because the old bridge was not far enough above the water for steam ships to pass, and as Front Street grew with river commerce, the East Bank grew as a center for lumber and planing mills and furniture manufacturers. Notice the logs in the river. The white building seen to the left of the bridge is the Edgefield and Nashville Manufacturing Company, founded in 1869. The grounds of the plant covered about 20 acres, and they manufactured "bank store, and office furniture, mantles, and other interior decorations." (TSLA.)

WOODLAND STREET, LOOKING WEST, 1905. This part of Woodland was known as Bridge Avenue until the trolley tracks turned at this intersection. This side street delineated manufacturing and residential parts of the neighborhood. The large brick building is the National Casket Company. Note the round horse watering trough in the road. (TSLA.)

WOODLAND STREET, LOOKING EAST, 1905. At this point, Bridge Avenue became Woodland Street, and, although some office buildings are evident, the area becomes increasingly more residential. This photograph was taken as a court exhibit for a case involving a traffic accident. (TSLA.)

94

J.W. Grimes Grocery, Woodland and Twelfth, about 1915. There was a Grimes Grocery at Twelfth and Woodland and at Sixteenth and Woodland. The Empress Theatre, an early nickelodeon, was on the other side of this building. (MNA.)

J.W. GRIMES GROCERY. Notice all the interesting signage in use and the elaborate house on the corner. This building was later used as the Nashville Photo Shop. (MNA.)

J.W. GRIMES, INTERIOR. Grimes was a grocery, soda fountain, and candy shop. This was before self-service grocery shopping. The clerk would write up your order and then collect and bag the goods you selected. (MNA.)

H.G. Hill Grocery, about 1930. H.G. Hill Grocery was located at Sixteenth and Fatherland Street. Opened in 1920, it operated for about 20 years. (H.G. Hill Company.)

J.W. Grimes Grocery, Sixteenth and Woodland, about 1920. When built, this building housed the business of Albert H. Goodall, grocer, and the Goodalls lived in the house attached. The building housed the J.W. Grimes Grocery from 1913 until the late 1920s, when the house and this space were enlarged and modernized into two storefronts. (LSNA.)

LEHNING BROTHERS' MEAT MARKET, ABOUT 1920. Lehning Brothers' Meat Market, founded in 1919, was located in the rear of the H.G. Hill Grocery at Tenth and Woodland (now a body shop). Pictured are H.W. Lehning, Ed Lehning Sr., and Mrs. Bennett. (Bud Lehning.)

LEHNING BROTHERS' GROCERY, 1940S. Located at 1012 Woodland Street, Lehning Brothers' Grocery operated until the mid-1980s. (Bud Lehning.)

LEHNING BROTHERS' GROCERY, INTERIOR. This photograph shows both how much changed and how much stayed the same between the time this photograph and the Grimes Grocery photograph was made. While the shopping cart indicates that shopping is now self-service, customers could still expect very personal attention from their neighborhood grocer. Shown are Doug Duncan, H.W. Lehning Sr. (behind meat counter), and Bobby Lehning. (Bud Lehning.)

THE WOODLAND THEATER, 1920. The Woodland advertised itself as "Nashville's Ace Suburban Theater, Complete Change of Program Three Times a Week." Since being converted to the Woodland Sound Studio in 1964, Barbara Mandrell, Johnny Cash, Charlie Daniels, Kansas, and others have recorded there. (TSLA.)

VESTER'S BILLIARDS, 1935. Vester's Billiards was located in the basement of the Vester home at the corner of Woodland and Eleventh and was operated by James Vester from the late 1920s until about 1938. The Vesters also owned the two houses next door. Gene Vester later opened another Vester's Billiards in the commercial building two doors up Eleventh (now Adex Realty). (James Vester Jr.)

ELEVENTH STREET, BETWEEN FORREST AND WOODLAND, 1940S. This commercial strip was in the area we now call Five Points. Country Egg & Poultry Company is to the left, the Varsity Cafe is in the middle, and the ice house and entrance to Vester's Billiards is in the rear of the house to the right. A Texaco service station occupies this block today. Note the trolley tracks on Eleventh Street. (James Vester Jr.)

NASHVILLE PHOTO SERVICE, 1951. This is the same building which had been Grimes Grocery and the Empress Theater early in the century. The Woodmen of the World met in the large room upstairs. Notice the small house where the post office is today. By this time, Vester's Billiards had been replaced with the Texaco Service Station. (MNA.)

FLUTY'S SERVICE CENTER, 1930. This small service station, next to the Woodland Theater, was one of the first in East Nashville. Mrs. Ashbough's Candy Shop was next door. On the other side of the theater was Patterson's Barber Shop and Mrs. Taylor's Beauty Shop. (MNA.)

HOOSER'S PHARMACY, 1948. Hooser's Pharmacy was an institution on the corner of Woodland and Fourteenth Streets. The pharmacy and soda fountain were in operation for about 65 years. Shown behind the soda fountain are "Uncle Dave" Hooser, Kay, Billy Cole, "Moma Hooser" and Little Billy, Dr. Stacy, and Billy Ledbetter. (Mae Hill.)

WOODLAND STREET, 1962. This photograph is of the northeast corner of Fourth and Woodland and was taken just beyond the bridge of the new interstate. It shows the changes in the street in an 80-year period, from Victorian mansion, to having shops built in the front lawn in the 1920s, to having the interstate and Urban Renewal transform the commercial landscape to a more suburban model. The mansion with storefronts in front was eventually razed to provide a parking lot for the adjacent building, which in recent years has been used as a thrift shop. The two-story building just beyond was the commissary for the Genesco Shoe Factory located on Main Street. (TSLA.)

Six

THE PARKS

East Nashville is blessed with several lovely parks. One of the earliest parks in the area was Fatherland Park, a neighborhood playground at Fatherland and Tenth Streets given by the city council to the Park Board in 1909. The playground was open until 1920, by which time the park system had expanded and the Park Board began to close neighborhood playgrounds. The East YMCA was built on this property in 1939 and is today used as a Head Start Center.

The largest park in East Nashville, and one of the earliest parks in the city, is Shelby Park. Shelby Park was operated as a private amusement park early in the century, but the company went bankrupt in 1903. The Park Board purchased the first 151 acres in 1909 and an additional 80 acres in 1911, with additional acreage added over time. The park opened to the public on July 4, 1912. Designed by Major E.C. Lewis, Shelby featured a number of interesting structures, including a full-size Dutch windmill, a boathouse shaped like the front of a riverboat, pergolas, log structures, and a Spanish Colonial Revival-style rest house. Dr. A.S. Keim of the YMCA organized the first city park baseball league in Shelby Park in 1915. The first Municipal Golf Course in Nashville was built on an additional 50-acre tract purchased between 1923 and 1927. The swimming pool at Shelby, built in the early 1930s also in the Spanish Colonial Revival style, was used by the Army for river assault boat training, and the riverfront was used for moorage by the U.S. Coastguard during World War II.

East Park was developed in the aftermath of the March 22, 1916 fire in Edgefield. This was the first effort of the Park Board to combine Park and school development programs, as Warner School was rebuilt at the same time. Park Commissioner Robert T. Creighton prepared the park plans, with fountain, flower beds, and walks radiating from a cut-stone beaux-arts-style bandstand designed by Donald W. Southgate. The park was doubled in size as part of the Urban Renewal in the early 1960s. The bandstand was razed in 1956, when a Quonset hut was placed in the park for use as a community center.

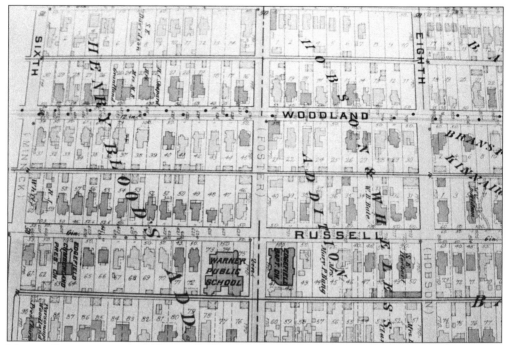

MAP OF EDGEFIELD, 1908. Notice the houses between Woodland and Russell. The 600 block of both streets would burn in the 1916 fire, and East Park would be developed on the site. The next block was cleared as part of Urban Renewal in 1963, and the park expanded to double its original size.

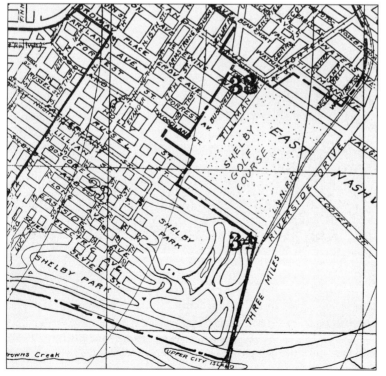

MAP OF SHELBY PARK, 1932. Note that Skyview Drive, Shady Lane, and much of the area we know as "Little Hollywood" had not yet been developed. These areas do, however, appear on a 1940 map.

ENTRANCE TO SHELBY PARK, 1913. This is the entrance to the park through Meredith Grove. The area west of this is now industrial, but was obviously rural at the time. The Park Board purchased 80 acres from J.R. Meredith in 1911. Note the Sycamore Lodge in the center and the tower for the water works to the right. (MPD.)

ENTRANCE TO SHELBY AT NINETEENTH STREET, ABOUT 1915. Small trees and shrubs are thickly planted at this main park entrance. One could ride the streetcar to this point and walk into the park. (MPD.)

SHELBY PARK. When Shelby Park opened on July 4, 1912, it was mostly a natural area of forest-covered wilderness, and the Park Board initially limited development. They opened a rock quarry to manufacture crushed stone to pave some 5 miles of roads. Over the years, land has been developed with more roads, playgrounds, and baseball fields. (MPD.)

RAILROAD BRIDGE, ABOUT 1915. This is the railroad bridge, in a view taken from the side we now know as Shelby Bottoms. (MPD.)

THE MULE BARN IN MEREDITH GROVE, 1920s. This is where maintenance equipment was kept for the park. (MPD.)

THE MISSION HOUSE, ABOUT 1920. The Mission House was one rest house for the park, and the Sycamore Lodge was another. Designed in the Spanish Colonial Revival style by E.C. Lewis, the Mission House had porches and a lounge area. (MPD.)

THE MISSION HOUSE. The House was located farther into the park than the current community center. The swimming pool, opened in 1931, was also of the Spanish style. (MPD.)

THE INTERIOR OF THE MISSION HOUSE. Appropriately, the Mission House at Shelby Park was furnished with Mission-style furniture, which was inexpensive, yet durable. This rugged oak furniture was popular early in the century because it hearkened back to an earlier time of simplicity and craftsmanship. (MPD.)

THE JACKSON CABIN, 1915. Several log cabins were constructed in the park. Notice the park benches and the simple stools constructed of logs. Several log picnic shelters are still in use. (MPD.)

THE SYCAMORE LODGE, ABOUT 1915. The Sycamore Lodge was one of the most memorable structures in the park. Constructed of cedar logs, the lodge offered restroom facilities, as well as a large room which was rented out for picnics and church and family gatherings. A porte-cochere is attached to the side. In 1984, the lodge was disassembled and moved to the Boxwell Reservation in Gallatin for use by a Boy Scout troop. (MPD.)

BARR-HIME CO.
NASHVILLE

WINDMILL HILL, 1920. Major E.C. Lewis also designed the Dutch windmill which sat atop "Windmill Hill." Built for the 1912 park opening, this windmill was said to be an exact full-scale replica of a windmill in Holland. One could climb the stairs to the high walk-around balcony, and sometimes see the "works" inside the shaft. (MPD.)

WINDMILL HILL, 1920. The windmill overlooked the playground, and was just below and across the road from the Municipal Iris Garden. It burned in the early 1940s, but the stone steps are still visible leading up to the hilltop on which it stood. (MPD.)

LAKE SEVIER. This view of Lake Sevier, with the windmill on the left and the boathouse on the right, was reproduced as a postcard. (MPD.)

BOATHOUSE ON LAKE SEVIER, 1930S. This fanciful boathouse, designed of wood and concrete to look like the front of a riverboat, was where one could rent paddle boats and canoes. The upper level also offered a great view of the lake and surrounding area. (MPD.)

THE CAVE SPRING, ABOUT 1920. There are seven springs on the park grounds, including the Cave Spring, Spout Spring, and Ebb & Flow. Here a lone woman enjoys the solitude of the Cave Spring. (MPD.)

THE CAVE SPRING, ABOUT 1920. Here we see a group outing to the Cave Spring, perhaps on a Sunday afternoon. Notice the fountain in the front. The Cave Spring can still be seen behind the community center, although the concrete has deteriorated through the years. (MPD.)

FISHING TOURNAMENT IN SHELBY PARK, 1956. Fishing tournaments on Lake Sevier have always been popular. This one was sponsored by the Fraternal Order of Police. (MNA.)

SHELBY PARK REGRADING, 1959. Shelby Park has changed and developed over time. Recently, new walks were built around the lake, trees were planted, a trail was built from the community center, and the 800-acre Shelby Bottoms Greenway was opened. (MNA.)

SHELBY PARK COMMUNITY CENTER, 1961. The Center was opened in 1961, after being funded in a 1958 bond issue. Although it lacks the charm of the Mission House or Sycamore Lodge, it has become a special place for picnics, volleyball games, and symphony concerts in the park. (MNA.)

East Park Being Laid Out, 1916. To the right, rubble can be seen where burned-out homes were cleared. Edgefield Baptist can be seen in the distance. (MPD.)

Aerial View of Edgefield, 1920s. The formal plan for East Park, with sidewalks radiating from the bandstand, can be seen. (NR.)

THE EAST PARK BANDSTAND, 1920s. The City Park Board purchased this land from Whitefoord R. Cole, president of the Nashville, Chattanooga, and St. Louis Railway. The surrounding gardens were developed with various flower beds, shrubs, and lily ponds. (MPD.)

NELLIE MCDOUGAL AND FRIENDS. This group is enjoying a day in East Park, 1920s. (TSLA.)

THE BEAUTIFUL CUT-STONE BEAUX-ARTS-STYLE BANDSTAND IN EAST PARK. The bandstand was designed by Donald W. Southgate, who also designed West End United Methodist Church, West End High School, Inglewood Baptist Church, and St. George's Episcopal Church. (MPD.)

BANDSTAND WITH PLAYGROUND IN FOREGROUND, 1950S. By the 1950s, the formal gardens had given way to playgrounds and grassy fields. Note the boy with the cigarette to the left. The bandstand was razed in 1956. East Park was doubled in size as part of Urban Renewal, and the ball field was added. (MPD.)

A FINAL WORD

The latest images in this book are from around 1961, and unfortunately, this marks the beginning of hard times for East Nashville. Many long-term residents began to move away to the suburbs, a trend repeated in other neighborhoods and cities. Many of the fine old homes were chopped into apartment buildings or torn down. Absentee owners, code violations, and halfway houses were plentiful. But in the mid-1970s, one of the most exciting periods in East Nashville's history began as people rediscovered its convenience and charm.

Edgefield was the first neighborhood in the city to be listed on the National Register of Historic Places. Parts of Lockeland Springs and East-End were also listed in the early 1980s as the East Nashville Historic District. Zoning overlays were put in place to protect the architectural character of the districts. The area was downzoned to discourage conversion of single-family homes to apartments, and active neighborhood associations were formed, which lobbied to stop a housing development from being built on the Shelby Park Golf Course and a landfill from being built on what is now Shelby Bottoms Greenway. The Holly Street Firehall, the Blind Girls' Home, and countless other buildings were saved by activist neighborhood groups. Today, homes in East Nashville are selling as quickly as other parts of the city, and values have appreciated significantly. Homes tours are held to show off rehabilitated homes, beautiful churches, and interesting corner stores and institutional buildings. Neighborhood associations sponsor monthly meetings with speakers, Neighborhood Watch programs, and tree planting and alley clean-up days. A coffeehouse, diner, florist, produce market, bakery, and art gallery have all opened in historic commercial corners in recent years, and plans for two new restaurants were announced recently.

East Nashville is the city's architectural treasure trove. Despite significant losses to natural disasters and Urban Renewal, the largest concentration of Victorian and early 20th-century architecture in the city can be found here. East Nashville is, without a doubt, Nashville's biggest preservation success story.

PEOPLE WALKING ACROSS THE FROZEN CUMBERLAND RIVER, 1940. I wanted to end with this image for two reasons. One is because it reflects the industrial heritage of the East Bank, which is changing after more than one hundred years. The Bridge Company is gone and an NFL stadium is now rising on the site. The second reason I like this image is what it represents. Earlier this year, when East Nashville was hit by another tornado, thousands of volunteers

crossed the river to help with clean-up. These volunteers discovered a strong community, physically damaged, but holding firm—neighborhoods of friendly and thankful people. As part of the NFL project, the Shelby Avenue Bridge will be preserved as a vital link to East Nashville and to the Shelby Bottoms Greenway. I hope people take the opportunity more and more in the years ahead to cross the river into East Nashville. (NR.)

ABOUT THE AUTHOR

E. Michael Fleenor has an M.A. in Public History and Historic Preservation from Middle Tennessee State University and is employed by the Tennessee Historical Commission as an historic preservation specialist working with state-owned historic sites and house museums. Fleenor is on the Board of Directors of Historic Nashville, Inc., Nashville's not-for-profit historic preservation organization. He edited *The Economic Benefits of Maintaining Community Character: Case Studies from Fredericksburg, Virginia and Galveston, Texas* for the National Trust for Historic Preservation, Department of Public Policy, and is a contributor to *The Tennessee Encyclopedia of History and Culture*, published by the Tennessee Historical Society.

BIBLIOGRAPHY

Brandaugh, Roberta Seawell. *History of Homes and Gardens of Tennessee*. Nashville, TN: The Garden Study Club, 1936, reprint 1964.

Caldwell, May Winston. *Beautiful and Historical Homes In and Near Nashville, Tennessee*. Nashville, TN: Brandon Publishing Co., 1911.

Clarke, Ida Clyde Gallagher, *All About Nashville: A Complete Historical Guidebook to the City*. Nashville, TN: Marshall & Bruce Co., 1912.

Clements, Paul. *A Past Remembered: A Collection of Antebellum Houses in Davidson County, Volume II*. Nashville, TN: Clearview Press, 1987.

Cornman, John. *Nashville: An Illustrated Review of its Progress and Importance*. Nashville, TN: Enterprise Publishing Company.

Crew, H.W. *History of Nashville, Tennessee*. Nashville, TN: Publishing House of the Methodist Episcopal Church, South, 1890.

Doyle, Don. *Nashville In the New South, 1880–1930*. Knoxville, TN: The University of Tennessee Press, 1985.

Edwards, Amelia Whitsett and Whitsett, Amelia Parker. *Growing Up in Edgefield*. Nashville, TN: J.M. Productions, Inc., 1998.

Egerton, John. *Nashville: The Faces of Two Centuries, 1780–1980*. Nashville,TN: PlusMedia, 1979.

First Church of the Nazarene. *Moments in History: 1898–1989*. Nashville, TN: First Church of the Nazarene, 1989.

Gower, Harry V.L. *Lockeland*. Nashville, TN: Harry V.L. Gower, unpublished remembrances, n.d.

Graham, Eleanor. *Nashville: A Short History and Selected Buildings*. Nashville, TN: Metropolitan Historical Commission, 1974.

Johnson, Leland R. *The Parks of Nashville: A History of the Board of Parks and Recreation*. Nashville, TN: Metro Board of Parks and Recreation, 1986.

Metropolitan Historical Commission. *Andrew Jackson Slept Here*. Nashville, TN: Metropolitan Historical Commission, 1993.

Morrison, Andrew. *The City of Nashville*. St. Louis, MO: George W. Engelhardt & Co., 1892.

Norman, Jack, Sr. *The Nashville I Knew*. Nashville, TN: Rutledge Hill Press, 1984.

Robert, Charles Edwin. *Nashville City Guide Book, Issued Under Authority of the Board of Directors, Centennial Commission*. Nashville, TN: Wheeler Brothers, 1880.

Thomason, Philip. *A Preservation Study of the East End and Lockeland Springs Neighborhoods of Nashville, TN*. Murfreesboro, TN: M.A. Thesis, Middle Tennessee State University, 1981.

Waller, William. *Nashville In the 1890s*. Nashville, TN: Vanderbilt University Press, 1970.

Waller, William. *Nashville, 1900–1910*. Nashville, TN: Vanderbilt University Press, 1972.

Zibart, Carl F. *Yesterday's Nashville*. Miami, FL: E.A. Seeman Publishing, 1976.